# CONTENTS

# Introduction

Reading and writing seem the most natural things in the world. However, it took thousands of years for people to devise ways of representing the sounds of speech in a written form. Many early peoples, like the ancient Egyptians, used systems of writing in which one symbol stood for a whole word. Systems like these were hard to learn, because there are hundreds of thousands of words in every language. And the symbols were difficult to draw because many of them were like tiny pictures of the objects they stood for. So the big breakthrough was to split words up into letters and invent the alphabet, something that first happened in the eastern Mediterranean about 3,600 years ago.

There was still no paper to write on, however. Different peoples used clay, papyrus, bark and animal skins as writing materials. Paper was invented in China around 1,000 years ago and did not reach the West for centuries after that. Once there was paper, inventors began to look for ways of printing words on this material. This meant the coming together of several different industries to produce presses, metal printing type and paper, to enable the next great revolution in communications, the printed book, to appear in Europe in the fifteenth century.

With the arrival of printing, books no longer had to be laboriously copied by hand. Knowledge could spread quickly and cheaply, and information flowed freely around Europe and beyond. Most of the later inventions in communications have had a similar effect. For example, radio, sound recording, film and television all reproduce information in different forms and allow more and more people to access it. In turn, each of these innovations has changed the world by bringing both knowledge and entertainment to millions.

This trend is continuing into the twenty-first century with the growth of computing and

the use of the internet. In the past few years, everything from vast libraries of information to movies and music files has been available online, bringing whole worlds to your screen. Computer programmers have supported this with tools such as search engines and music players that make all this information increasingly easier to find and use. As a result, our era is truly an age of communication, and one that looks set to continue long into the future.

**PHILIP WILKINSON**

# LETTERS & SIGNS

*From its beginning as a simple system for keeping records, writing has developed so that it can be used to record and pass on everything from short messages to the most complex information.*

History could only truly begin once a system of writing things down had been developed. Before that, people had to rely on word of mouth to pass on information. They could only learn as much as older people remembered about the past.

Stories became jumbled and were only shared among members of a family or group, so future generations have had to guess and piece together conflicting pieces of information about this time. Once writing had been developed, the way was open for people to record their thoughts and observations and to detail the history of their civilization, its way of life, customs and religion.

However, writing was not invented for these reasons. It began as a means of recording official matters such as taxes and payments for trading goods. Writing was first developed by the ancient Sumerians

△ *Sumerian clay tablet.*

▷ *A reed stylus was used to make the wedge-shaped symbols of Sumerian cuneiform writing. The three scripts shown in the foreground are Egyptian, Roman and Chinese.*

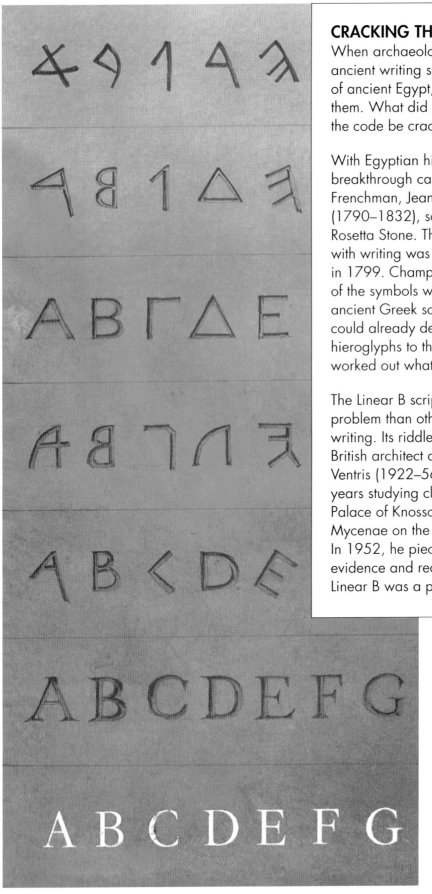

## CRACKING THE CODE

When archaeologists first discovered ancient writing such as the hieroglyphs of ancient Egypt, they were baffled by them. What did they mean? How could the code be cracked?

With Egyptian hieroglyphs, the breakthrough came in 1822, when a Frenchman, Jean François Champollion (1790–1832), solved the mystery of the Rosetta Stone. This slab of stone covered with writing was found by French soldiers in 1799. Champollion realized that some of the symbols were repeated in an ancient Greek script which scholars could already decipher. By matching the hieroglyphs to the Greek letters, he worked out what the writing said.

The Linear B script presented more of a problem than other forms of Greek writing. Its riddle was worked out by a British architect and scholar, Michael Ventris (1922–56). Ventris spent ten years studying clay tablets found at the Palace of Knossos on Crete and at Mycenae on the mainland of Greece. In 1952, he pieced together the evidence and realized that the Minoan Linear B was a primitive form of Greek.

◁ *These examples show how the alphabet developed from the Phoenician script to the modern Roman alphabet we use today. The Romans adopted the Greek alphabet from the Etruscans who ruled over central Italy from 800 to 200 BC. The Latin script used in the Roman Empire has hardly changed in nearly 2,000 years.*

in Mesopotamia about 5,500 years ago. These early writings were marks scratched on to limestone tablets. In about 3000 BC, scribes in Mesopotamia began to write on soft clay tablets which were then baked hard in the sun.

At first, the writing itself was in the form of pictures. A simple picture or symbol represented each object. This system was laborious because scribes had to master more than 2,000 symbols for the words they needed. It was also difficult to provide any descriptive information about the objects they were illustrating. So scribes introduced less rigid symbols, known as 'ideographs'. A single symbol not only represented an object but also ideas connected with it. For example, a circle could mean either the sun, light, warmth or daylight.

## CUNEIFORM

It still took a long time to produce writing by this method because it was difficult to make recognizable drawings with a 'stylus', the writing implement used by the scribes. This was made of reed or wood, and had a wedge-shaped tip. Gradually, a more abstract system of simple wedge-shaped symbols made with the tip of the stylus developed. This was known as 'cuneiform' writing, from the Greek for 'wedge-shaped'.

The Mesopotamians began to use these symbols to show sounds as well as objects, and to string sounds together to make whole words. For example, if you were putting together the word 'belief' in cuneiform, you would use the symbol for 'bee' and the symbol for 'leaf', even though these words have nothing to do with the word they are spelling. Even with this new system, however, scribes still had to learn about 600 symbols, so very few people could read or write.

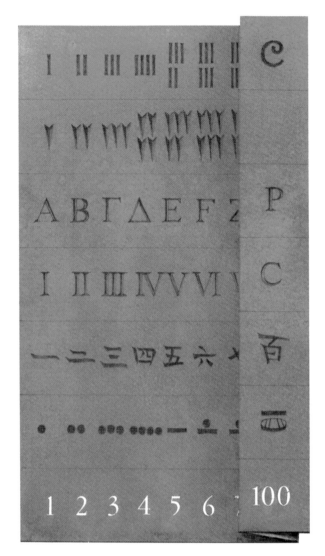

△ *The earliest form of counting was to use fingers and thumbs, but as trading progressed, a more formal system was needed to record numbers. The Egyptians and Babylonians used strokes grouped together. The Maya grouped dots. The Greeks adapted alphabet symbols and the Romans used a mixture of strokes and letters. Modern numbers evolved from early Indian numbers.*

Cuneiform was also adopted as a writing system by the Babylonians, the Persians and the Assyrians, although their languages were very different. Most early tablets are tax records and details of ownership and sales, but from about 2400 BC, people began to use writing in more imaginative ways such as for poetry, letters and magic spells.

## HIEROGLYPHS

Meanwhile, the Egyptians were developing their own style of writing which was used from about 3000 BC. This is known as 'hieroglyphic' script. The writing was mainly used for inscriptions on buildings and tombs. Hieroglyphs were pictures, but they could be adapted in different ways. There were about 700 picture symbols which could be used to represent either the object they showed or words which sounded similar. They could also be put together as the syllables of a longer word. Twenty-four extra signs represented single consonant sounds, to write words that could not be illustrated.

Egyptian scribes gradually introduced a quicker, simpler writing called 'hieratic', although tomb inscriptions were still written in hieroglyphs.

Two civilizations in Mexico invented their own form of picture writing. The Maya, who lived on the Yucatán peninsula from AD 300, carved their picture symbols, or 'glyphs', on to huge stone pillars and also painted them on to long strips of bark paper which were folded into books. The Aztecs, who settled in Mexico in about 1325, used glyphs which were probably developed from the Mayan system, although they are easier to decipher.

## WRITING SOUNDS

All these picture symbols could be written in any direction, which made them even harder to understand. In Egypt, the reader was helped by the fact that the characters faced the way in which the pictures were meant to be read.

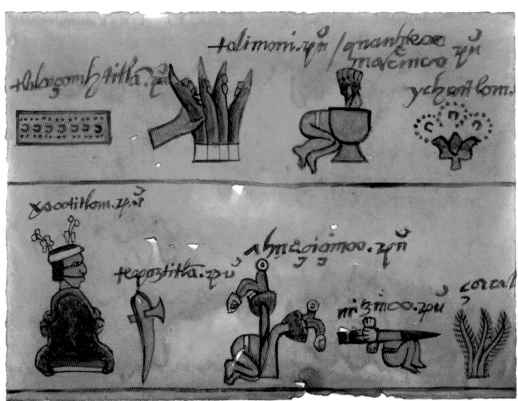

△ *The Aztecs of Mexico used a sophisticated picture script. Spanish translations are written in alongside.*

△ *A selection of scripts, from left to right: ancient Egyptian hieroglyphs; the Minoan Phaistos disc which has not yet been deciphered; Greek numerals; Roman letters; Arabic script; Chinese characters; Maya glyphs.*

These early forms of writing were difficult to master because there was a different symbol for every object or every syllable of a word. So there could be thousands of symbols to memorize, and it was beyond the skill of most people to learn how to read and write.

The big breakthrough in the history of writing came when people began to realize that all the syllables were made up of the same few sounds, and that each of these could be shown by a single symbol or letter. This discovery was made in about 1600 BC by the peoples who lived by the shores of the eastern Mediterranean. Their alphabets are known as 'Semitic' scripts.

The Canaanites, who lived in what is now Israel and Lebanon, developed an alphabet in which each symbol was named after the object it was based on. For example, the Canaanite word for 'ox' began with an 'a' sound, so the 'a' sound was represented by the head of an ox. The Phoenicians, who lived along the shores of the Mediterranean in Lebanon and Syria, adapted the Canaanite script for

their alphabet. They were a seafaring people, and their alphabet spread far and wide. But it contained only consonants, so it was more like shorthand than a true alphabet.

## WHICH WAY TO WRITE?

The Greeks adapted the Phoenician script but introduced vowels as well as consonants. New Greek scripts evolved as time went by. Two of these, known as 'Linear A' and 'Linear B', were used by the Minoans who lived on the island of Crete. These scripts were the first always to be written in horizontal lines.

At first, the Greeks wrote from right to left. Later, they wrote from right to left and from left to right on alternate lines, so the reader zigzagged back and forth. This style is known as 'boustrophedon' which means 'in the way an ox ploughs a field'. Finally, they settled on the system of writing from left to right, as we do today.

### AN UNSOLVED MYSTERY

The Greek Linear B script developed from an earlier form known as Linear A. This script is only found in about 400 inscriptions on clay tablets. In spite of numerous attempts to decipher it, Linear A remains an unsolved mystery.

*The Chinese wrote their characters with a brush and a cake of ink. The name written here says K'ung-Fu-tzu. This man is better known in Europe as Confucius (c. 552–479 BC), the great Chinese philosopher.*

## THE ALPHABET

The word 'alphabet' comes from 'alpha' and 'beta' which are the first two letters of the Greek alphabet. If you look at the classical Greek alphabet, you can see many similarities with the alphabet we use today. This is because the Roman alphabet used in many parts of the world was developed from the later version of the Greek alphabet. By this time, the Greeks had also adapted the way they wrote letters to suit the materials they were using. If letters were to be carved in stone, it was easier to have straight lines so the letters were pointed with sharp angles. For writing on papyrus or parchment however, a more rounded style flowed better. The Romans followed this through, changing angular Greek letters to rounded ones and also dropping some of the letters altogether. By the seventh century BC, the Roman alphabet had 21 letters. By about the first century BC, the letters Y and Z were added, and finally J, U and W were added in the Middle Ages. With the simplified alphabets of Greece and Rome, writing was within the grasp of everyone.

A different alphabet evolved in the East, although it, too, stemmed from the Semitic scripts of the eastern Mediterranean. This was 'Aramaic' and it probably first appeared in the tenth century BC. It is the ancestor of both Hebrew and Arabic scripts. Arabic is the language and script of the Koran, the holy book of the Islamic religion, so this script spread through followers of this faith. The modern 28-letter Arabic alphabet is written from right to left.

## ONE SCRIPT, MANY TONGUES

One form of writing stayed separate from the rest. This was Chinese, which does not have an alphabet but consists of thousands of symbols, or 'characters'.

Unlike other scripts, the Chinese system has become more complicated with time. During the Shang period (about 1766–1122 BC), there were about 2,500 signs. Today, there are about 50,000. Some of these are pictures of objects, some suggest abstract ideas. The writing is difficult to learn but it has an advantage in China, where many languages are spoken.

With other scripts, if you see writing in a foreign language, even though you recognize the alphabet, you cannot understand the words unless you know that language. But, as Chinese writing represents a word with symbols instead of spelling it out, people do not have to speak the same language to understand it. In 1979, the Chinese introduced an alphabet of 58 letters used for writing proper names and place names.

The Chinese style of writing spread throughout the Far East. Japan adopted it in the third century AD, but it was not ideally suited to their language. Five hundred years later, they developed a script which was broken down into syllables. This new script meant that

fewer symbols had to be memorized. Today, there are two styles of writing in Japan, one for official documents and one for literature. Each has only 50 symbols. And so, through people's need to record details of trading, religious beliefs, as well as their thoughts and imaginative ideas in the form of literature, the concept of writing spread throughout the world.

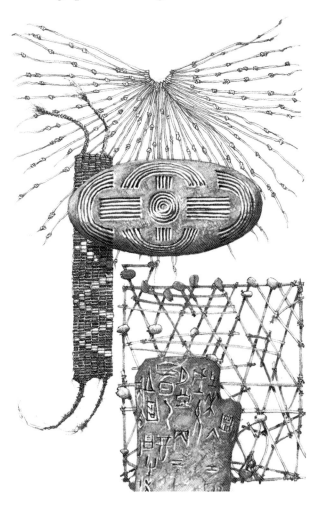

△ *Some societies did not use writing to communicate. The Incas of Peru used the 'quipu', in which different coloured cords were knotted in various ways to record information. The Iroquois Indians of North America used patterns and colours on their wampum belts to pass on information. The Aborigines of Australia used message sticks in which marks or grooves were cut. In medieval England, sticks with notches cut in them were still used to record financial matters, even though written scripts were widespread by then.*

# THE BOOK

*Today, we can find books on almost any subject, but it took centuries to arrive at a quick, cheap way of printing them. The first books were so precious that only a few people were ever allowed to touch them.*

O ur world is full of books, magazines and all sorts of printed materials. We can read to learn or for pleasure. We can find books to help us with everyday living or show us the beauty of the world around us. There can be no subject in the world that people have not written about at some time. However, in the days of the early civilizations, it was a very different story. The book developed in stages over thousands of years before the invention of the printing press made books available to everyone.

Early clay tablets were not a very practical material for producing books. They were unwieldy to read and storage was a problem. Even so, a few ancient writings have been found on clay tablets. The most ancient poem of all, the *Epic of Gilgamesh*, was found on 12 clay tablets in the library of King Assurbanipal of Assyria (669–627 BC), although the poem was written long before his reign. Gilgamesh was a legendary king of Uruk in Mesopotamia.

△ *Records written on papyrus scrolls could be stored for a long time in Egypt's dry climate.*

The poem tells of his adventures trying to find the secret of eternal life. The tablets were written in Akkadian script, a type of cuneiform writing which was developed after King Sargon of Akkad (c. 2334–2279 BC) came to the Assyrian throne in 2300 BC.

When archaeologists excavated the Royal Palace at Ebla in the Near East, they discovered a library of 1,900 clay tablets dating back to about 2000 BC. These tablets record over 140 years of Ebla's history. Findings of this kind are rare, however. Before writers could let their imaginations have free reign in the creation of literature, better writing materials had to be introduced.

*King Assurbanipal of Assyria.*

## PORTABLE PAPYRUS

The first stage was to find a less cumbersome surface to write on than clay tablets. In about 3500 BC, the ancient Egyptians discovered that the papyrus reed which grew by the River Nile could be made into a type of paper. The reed grows to three metres tall, and has thick triangular stems filled with a white spongy pith.

The Egyptians removed the green outer skin and cut the pith into thin strips of equal length. They laid the strips side by side, with their edges overlapping, to make a sheet of the size they wanted. Then they laid another layer of strips at right-angles to the first layer. The layers were dampened and pressed under a heavy weight, or hammered flat. As the fibres dried, they knitted together to form a thin sheet of writing material also known as 'papyrus', which gives us the English word 'paper'. Scribes wrote on papyrus with a reed pen dipped in ink. The earliest types of ink were made from water mixed with vegetable gum and soot or vegetable dye.

▽ *Books have long been used to spread all kinds of knowledge, from the scientific discoveries of ancient Greece to the religious writings of the Middle Ages. When printing was invented, more books were written for entertainment, such as poetry and stories.*

*▽ Early books were not made of sheets bound together as they are today. The first books came in the form of clay tablets, and later books were in the form of rolls of papyrus, silk or parchment.*

Papryus soon became the most common type of writing material in Egypt and continued to be used for thousands of years. It was exported from Egypt to other Mediterranean lands and later civilizations, such as the Greeks and the Romans, made their own papyrus from imported reeds. The disadvantage of using papyrus was that the papyrus reed only grew wild in Egypt, so everyone had to rely on only one source of writing material. If Egypt stopped supplying it for some reason, then scribes throughout the civilized world would have nothing to write on. So a new type of material was developed.

## A NEW MATERIAL

'Parchment' was made from sheep, goat or calf skin. A more delicate version, 'vellum', was made from the skins of very young animals. Eumenes, King of Pergamon in Asia Minor (197–159 BC) is said to have invented parchment in the second century BC. Legend has it that the pharaoh of Egypt stopped supplying papyrus because he was jealous of the library at Pergamon and wanted to stop new books being added to it. Refusing to be thwarted, Eumenes turned his mind to finding a new material for his scribes to write on. The name 'parchment' is said to come from the word 'Pergamon'.

Parchment and vellum were made by soaking the animal skins in lime, and then stretching them and scraping them clean. The skin was rubbed with a pumice stone until it was perfectly smooth.

Parchment was the main writing material until well into the Middle Ages. People wrote on it with a quill pen made from a goose feather. This combination was so successful that medieval monks could produce exquisite illuminated manuscripts in which letters were decorated with designs in gold, silver and brilliant colours. The sheets of parchment were sewn together to make books protected by covers made from leather or wood. And so the book as we know it began to appear.

## PAPER-MAKING

In the East, writing materials were developing in different ways. In China, people wrote with the same type of brush that they used for painting. In fact, writing and painting were often combined, particularly in poetry. Early books were produced on rolls of silk or strips of bamboo. But the Chinese were also responsible for one of the most important developments in the history of the book. This was the invention of paper.

Paper was first made in China in about AD 50. Old fishing nets, hemp and rags were beaten in water until they were a pulp of fibres. The pulp was spread on to a bamboo screen. The water drained through the screen, leaving a mat of fibres. Then, all the water was pressed out of the fibres and the paper was dried in the sun.

*Medieval books were decorated with elaborate coloured or 'illuminated' initials.*

It was several hundred years before the secret of paper-making reached the West, and even then it happened quite by chance. The city of Samarkand in Uzbekistan was the main junction of the Silk Road, the ancient trading route between China and the Mediterranean. During the Siege of Samarkand in AD 768, Arabs conquered the city and captured many Chinese prisoners of war. Among these prisoners were paper-makers who passed on the secret of their craft.

The Arabs began to develop their own paper-making industry which spread from Samarkand to other cities such as Baghdad, Damascus and Cairo. Paper-making skills reached Byzantium in the eleventh century and finally spread to western Europe in the twelfth century.

The development of books grew with the spread of paper-making. In AD 900, Baghdad had about 100 workshops where scribes copied books for sale. Centres of learning such as Toledo in Spain and Fez in Morocco were also paper-making centres where books were produced.

## PRINTING BLOCKS

Copying books by hand was a laborious business and, once again, it was in the East that the next development took place. During the ninth century, printed books began to appear in China. The text and pictures were carved on wooden blocks which were coated with ink. The blocks were then pressed on to paper to print the page. The Chinese also developed single pieces of type which could be moved around in different arrangements, but this was a very complicated system to use for Chinese writing, because separate blocks were needed for each of the thousands of different Chinese characters.

## RELIGIOUS BOOKLETS

The first printed books in Europe appeared in monasteries, where monks had been copying by hand for centuries. The monks used carved wood blocks to print the books. At first, blocks were simply made to print decorated letters which appeared often. Then, the monks began to print religious pictures with short texts and then short booklets. The monks printed these in the language of the country they were in instead of in Latin, the official language of the Roman Catholic Church that only priests and scholars could understand. Suddenly, it was possible to spread information to a wider audience.

The wood block method was satisfactory for printing short works, but it had disadvantages for longer books. A separate block had to be carved for each page, which took a long time, even when the work was done by skilled woodcarvers. Each block

▽ *Medieval monks spent much of their time copying books by hand. One book could take hundreds of hours of work.*

## WRITING THE BIBLE

The way the Bible came to be written is a good example of how early books were first written. The earliest versions of the Old Testament were written on scrolls of parchment. Many people contributed to the Old Testament and although most of it was written in Hebrew, two of the books were written in Aramaic. Scribes had to keep making new copies because the scrolls disintegrated as time went by. The Dead Sea Scrolls, found in a cave by a shepherd boy in 1947, are more than 2,000 years old and are the oldest copies of the Old Testament found so far.

The New Testament was written in Greek. The earliest books were written on scrolls of papyrus, but in later versions the paper was folded to make a 'codex'.

In Roman times, the Bible was written in Latin. Then, in the fourteenth century, scholars began to translate the Bible into other languages. In England, a scholar called John Wycliffe (c. 1329–84) made the first English translation.

Many English versions appeared after that, but the old-fashioned English of these older Bibles can be difficult for people to understand today. Modern versions rewrite the Bible using everyday language.

could only be used to print one page of one book, so a lot of time was wasted in carving blocks that would only be used for a small number of copies of a booklet. It was also difficult to carve the letters clearly enough to make a good impression on the page. Sometimes the wood warped which made the carving useless. So, before whole books could be produced, printers had to look for a more efficient method. The answer was to use metal instead of wood.

## MOVABLE TYPE

In the middle of the fifteenth century, metal-workers in different parts of Europe began to experiment with making metal type. Metal type was perfected in about 1450 by Johannes Gutenberg (c. 1400–68) who was born in the German town of Mainz.

He was a skilled goldsmith, but he was also fascinated by books. He would spend hours in the monastery library, studying the books and watching the monks copying them out by hand. He realized what a slow process this was, and wondered if metal-work could be used to produce the books more quickly. The idea came to him that the letters of the alphabet could be cast on separate blocks of metal, called 'movable type', which could be moved round to form words.

In 1428, Gutenberg moved to Strasbourg and set up in business with a partner, Johann Fust (1400–66), who was to put up the money for the equipment they needed. In 1456, they produced the first book printed with movable type, the famous Gutenberg Bible. But Fust wanted the business for himself and so he demanded his money back from Gutenberg. Gutenberg could not pay and was forced out of the business he had invented. In 1457, Fust printed a Psalter

*◁ The first printed books did not look very different from handwritten ones. The letters were shaped in the same handwritten style, known as Gothic script, and the pictures were printed from wood blocks and coloured by hand.*

or Book of Psalms, which was mainly Gutenberg's work.

After Gutenberg's invention, however, books became more widely available and printing industries were set up in many cities, including London, Paris, Rome, Venice, Florence, Milan and Cologne. Gutenberg had printed his book in Gothic type, which was an imitation of the handwriting used by the monks. By 1470, printers were using Roman type, with separate, upright letters, far easier to read than Gothic. The rounded, sloping letters of Italic type appeared in 1495.

## SPREADING IDEAS
By this time, a new period of learning had begun. The Middle Ages were followed

by the Renaissance or 'rebirth' of Europe. From the middle of the fourteenth century, there was new interest in the works of the ancient Greeks and Romans. The Renaissance began in Italy, where rich and powerful people, such as the Medici family, encouraged the work of painters, sculptors, poets and scholars.

## ASKING QUESTIONS

People became hungry for more knowledge and began to question the ideas of the past. They also began to question the behaviour of the all-powerful Roman Catholic Church which had been dominant for 1,000 years. This new awakening was helped by the invention of printing.

By 1500, there were printing presses in 143 European towns and more than 16,000 different works had been published. Counting all the different editions, such as separate editions of the

Bible produced by different printers, there were 40,000 printed titles. At first, most books were Bibles, prayer books and Psalters, but before long other books began to appear, such as translations of ancient Greek and Roman works and law and science books. Influential thinkers such as the Dutch scholar, Erasmus (1466–1536), could circulate their work to a wide audience through printing. Erasmus's work *In Praise of Folly*, published in 1509, attacked the Catholic Church for squeezing money out of its followers to line its own pockets.

▽ *Gutenberg's print shop was crowded and busy. On the right, the first printer is screwing the heavy press down on the paper which lies on top of the bed of type. The printer in the background is coating the type with ink. An ink dabber is shown in the centre foreground. On the left, letters are being removed from the wooden storage case and assembled in a line in a narrow frame known as a composing stick.*

Criticism of the Church led to another Renaissance movement, the Reformation. Rebellion against the domination of the Roman Catholic Church spread across Europe from about 1500. It was started by Martin Luther (1483–1546), who was born in Saxony. Luther, who had studied religion and become an Augustinian friar, went to Rome on a pilgrimage and was disgusted by what he saw. He told of priests who sold 'Indulgences', or pardons for sins, and so-called religious relics which were no more than animal bones. Printing helped his cause because he was able to publish pamphlets in their thousands. These pamphlets, urging people to rebel against the Church, were circulated throughout Europe and helped to end the dominance of the Roman Catholic Church.

In England, the first printing press was set up by William Caxton (c. 1422–91) in 1476. Caxton had learned the printing trade in Cologne and he produced about 80 titles at his printing press in London. England did not have the painters and sculptors of Italy, but it was famous for its playwrights and poets such as William Shakespeare (1564–1616) and Edmund Spenser (c. 1552–99). The first edition of all of Shakespeare's plays was published in 1623.

## POWER-DRIVEN PRESSES

In these early presses, the letters were assembled by hand. The problem was to keep the letters firmly in place while several copies were printed. After experimenting with various methods, printers came up with the idea of arranging the letters in a wooden frame called a 'forme'. The paper was pressed on to the letters from above. Everything was set up and operated by hand.

Faster printing became possible in the nineteenth century when power-driven presses were introduced. In the cylinder press, a cylinder rolled the paper over a flat surface which held the type. In the later rotary press, the type was also on a cylinder. In 1884, the Linotype system was invented. Instead of positioning each letter separately, the typesetter typed words for a whole line of type using a keyboard. A solid line of type was then formed from molten metal.

## MAKING IT LEVEL

Applying the ink was also a problem with the early presses. At first, ink was applied to the metal type with two circular 'dabbers'. The printer covered them with ink and then dabbed ink on to the type. It was difficult to coat the type thoroughly once it was arranged in the press, so the bed on which the type was laid was put

*△ By the nineteenth century, printers used these enormous presses. As many more people learned to read, books and newspapers flourished.*

on to a sliding carriage. The type could be slid out to be inked and then pushed back into the press.

If each piece of type was not perfectly level, some letters would not print properly. For example, if a letter was even slightly lower than the others, the paper would not come into contact with it when the press was applied. The answer was to put several sheets of paper under the sheet being printed. This allowed enough 'give' to push the paper on to each letter when pressure was applied.

Printing has continued to develop and become more sophisticated, but nothing achieved since has had the same impact as the invention of movable type, which opened the world of books to everyone.

# ACROSS THE WORLD

*Communication links between people have always been important, but we have moved a long way from the beacons and smoke signals used by early people to the fax machines and computers we have today.*

People have always needed to communicate with each other across long distances. Bonfires on hilltops were an early method of signalling danger. In ancient China, bonfires were lit along the Great Wall to warn of attacks from barbarians. The North American Indians used smoke signals. The Romans flashed messages with mirrors turned to catch the sunlight. Flashing lights and flags have been used in a similar way.

Sending messages in this way worked well in certain circumstances. However, the people receiving the signals had to be able to see them, so they had to be sent from a prominent viewpoint which was not too far away. If the messages were complicated, a code had to be used which had to be understood by everyone. Such signals were usually only used to send messages in times of war, but until the nineteenth century, the only other way of communicating was to send a written message, which took time if the people involved lived any distance apart.

△ *This is the very first telephone, which Bell used to speak to Tom Watson on 6 March 1876.*

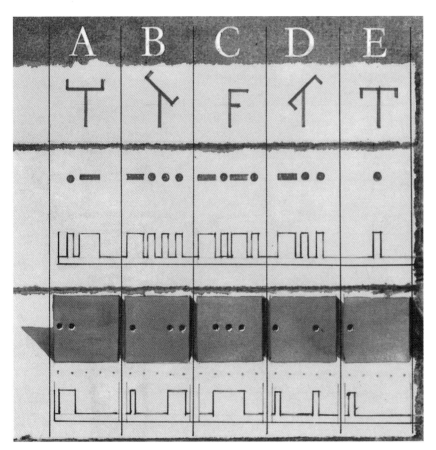

◁ *Semaphore code*
*Developed in 1794, semaphore used a system of moving arms worked by ropes to create symbols for each letter.*

◁ *Morse code*
*Samuel Morse's code could be transmitted along a wire using a key. The code is shown as dots and dashes and (below) as electrical signals.*

◁ *Five-unit code*
*This code was developed from Morse code. It was used with a teleprinter, an instrument for typing telegraphs that were sent along wires.*

## THE TELEGRAPH

Then, in the nineteenth century, a new discovery at last brought more efficient methods of communication.

In 1831, a British scientist, Michael Faraday (1791–1867), made the first electric generator. He found that moving a loop of wire over a magnet produced an electric current. He then tried moving the magnet instead of the wire and found that an electric current was produced again.

Once the link between electricity and magnetism had been established, it could be used in other ways. The first telegraph was patented by British scientist, Sir Charles Wheatstone (1802–75) and an Indian Army Officer, Sir William Cooke (1806–79), in 1837. It used magnetic needles which pointed at different letters in response to electric currents.

Another type of electric telegraph was developed by an American inventor,

△ *After the invention of the telegraph, telegraph wires spread all over the land, linking towns and cities, and changing the look of the countryside.*

△ *Alexander Graham Bell using his early telephone equipment. Behind are some of his rough sketches for his telephone.*

Samuel Morse (1791–1872). He devised 'Morse code', a system which could be tapped out on an electric key. The code for each letter was made up of a different combination of long buzzes or 'dashes', and short buzzes or 'dots'. The message was received by another machine at the other end of the telegraph line, where an operator decoded it. Morse code could also be transmitted with flashing lights. Morse established the first telegraph line between Washington and Baltimore in 1844. At last, there was an efficient way of sending messages quickly. By the 1860s, telegraph wires connected the East and West coasts of the United States and there was a cable across the Atlantic to Europe.

## TRANSMITTING VOICES

The telegraph was a big breakthrough but it still had disadvantages. The sender and the receiver had to understand Morse code, so messages had to be sent to telegraph offices where skilled operators decoded them. Then the message had to be delivered to the person concerned. It was quicker than sending a letter, but not as quick as being able to speak to the person directly. If coded messages could be sent along electric wires, could the human voice also be transmitted? It seemed a possibility to one man at least, Alexander Graham Bell (1847–1922).

Bell was born in Scotland where he lived until he was 23. His mother was deaf, and his father in specialized teaching deaf children. Bell also became a teacher of the deaf, and, when the family emigrated to Canada in 1870, he continued his work there. He moved to Boston, in Massachusetts, USA, three years later. His work with deaf children made him think about speech sounds and question whether they could be transmitted along electric wires like telegraphs, which by now were well established.

*On early telephones, such as Bell's 'box' telephone, the earpiece and mouthpiece were combined. There was no dial on these early phones. You had to call the operator to put your call through.*

## COME HERE, WATSON!

Bell knew that sounds make vibrations on the eardrum which the brain translates to make sense of them. His idea was to make a transmitter with a disc which would vibrate when struck by sound waves, in the same way as the eardrum. Sound vibrations from the transmitter would pass along a wire to a receiver which would also have a vibrating disc. This receiver would convert the sound vibrations back into words.

Bell spent two years making his transmitter. The breakthrough came in 1875 when Bell, listening on the receiver in one room, heard

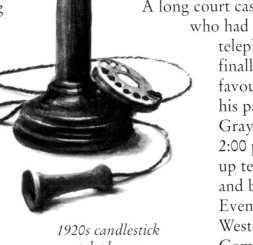

*1920s candlestick telephone.*

distinct sounds from his assistant, Watson, who was adjusting the transmitter in another room. Bell continued working on his calculations and, on 6 March 1876, he transmitted the first words, 'Come here, Watson, I want you.'

Watson, listening on the receiver in another part of the house, heard him. The telephone had been invented.

Bell patented his invention in 1876, and in the same year he made the first long-distance call between Brantford and Paris in Ontario, Canada, a distance of 110 kilometres. Now, it was only a matter of time before it would be possible to communicate by telephone with anywhere in the world.

## RIVAL INVENTORS

But Bell was not the only person who had come up with this idea. An American, Elisha Gray (1835–1901), was also developing a telephone quite independently of Bell. Gray patented his invention on the same day as Bell. A long court case followed to establish who had actually invented the telephone. The judges finally decided in Bell's favour because he had filed his patent at noon, and Gray had not filed his until 2:00 pm! Both men set up telephone companies and became bitter rivals. Eventually, Gray sold his Western Union Telegraph Company to Bell.

Bell had great success with his invention. He demonstrated it at exhibitions and people were interested in this new method of communication. The next problem was how to link up telephone lines so that people could ring up anyone they liked. The answer was a telephone exchange, where lines from different telephone subscribers could be plugged into a switchboard to connect them to each other.

The first telephone exchange was set up in 1878, in New Haven, Connecticut. It connected lines between 21 telephone subscribers in the New Haven area, one of whom was the writer, Mark Twain (1835–1910). By 1885, there were 140,000 subscribers and 800 telephone exchanges. The number of telephone subscribers and exchanges continued to grow in other countries across the world.

The early telephone exchanges were manual, which meant that operators sat in the exchange and plugged the lines into a switchboard by hand to connect calls. Today, callers can dial almost anywhere in the world without having to go through an operator. The calls are connected by computers.

## WIRELESS LINKS

The methods of communication developed so far relied on wires to link up transmitters and receivers. In the middle of the nineteenth century, scientists began to examine the idea of transmitting sounds without wires.

The first man to introduce the idea of electromagnetic waves was the British scientist, James Clerk Maxwell (1831–79), who demonstrated that light is an electromagnetic wave and suggested the

◁ *Guglielmo Marconi with his equipment for making radio transmissions.*

△ *Radios on board ships meant that even during a long ocean voyage, the passengers and crew were not cut off completely from land or from other ships.*

idea of radio waves. In 1888, German scientist, Heinrich Hertz (1857–94) produced and detected radio waves with a simple transmitter.

## MARCONI'S IDEAS

But the person who actually invented the wireless, or radio as we call it today, was an Italian electrical engineer, Guglielmo Marconi (1874–1937). In 1894, Marconi read a newspaper report describing electromagnetic waves which travelled through space at 300,000 kilometres a second. He resolved to find out if these 'wireless' waves could be used to transmit sound. At first, he worked in a makeshift workshop in his parents' villa near Bologna. He built a simple transmitter and managed to detect radio waves.

Marconi realized that he could send transmissions over longer distances with a more powerful transmitter and receiver. A Russian scientist, Aleksandr Popov (1859–1905), was also studying radio waves, although he used them to detect distant thunderstorms and not for communication. In 1895, Popov discovered that a long vertical wire on the receiver made it more sensitive to the signals, and so invented the aerial. Marconi made use of this invention by fitting aerials to his transmitter and receiver. He worked on his invention until he managed to send a signal from the house to a field two kilometres away.

## ACROSS THE AIR-WAVES

Tremendously excited by his discovery, Marconi offered his invention to the Italian Ministry of Posts and Telegraphs.

between Dover on the English coast and Wimereux near Boulogne on the French coast. In 1901, with the help of an Englishman, Sir John Fleming (1849–1945), he made his first radio link across the Atlantic between Cornwall and Newfoundland.

So far, radio messages had been sent in Morse code. The human voice was first heard on the radio in the United States just before the World War I. Marconi had formed his own wireless company by this time and he continued to develop

## HOW SOUND AND RADIO WAVES TRAVEL

Sounds are made by rapid vibrations, or sound waves, which the brain translates so that we can understand them. Sound waves spread out like ripples on water, becoming weaker as they get further from their source. Sound travels through the air at about 1,200 kilometres per hour.

Sound waves have to have something to travel through. They can travel through solid materials like walls as well as through air, but thicker materials absorb some of the sound. There is no sound in space because there is no air for it to travel through. Astronauts have to speak to each other by radio because radio waves can travel through space.

Electromagnetic waves such as light and radio waves travel faster than sound. To transmit sound by radio waves, a microphone in a transmitter converts them into electrical signals. The signals pass to an aerial in the transmitter and spread out as radio waves. The aerial on the receiver picks up the waves and a loudspeaker turns them back into sounds.

To his great disappointment, they were not interested, so he went to London to demonstrate his invention. The British Government were interested in his work, and asked him to give a demonstration to army and navy officers. Naval officers quickly saw the possibilities of wireless signals for shipping. In 1899, Marconi transmitted a message about 50 kilometres across the English Channel,

his invention. He was most interested in using radio for communication between specific groups, such as soldiers in the field or ships at sea. But his invention was soon to become a means of communicating to a far wider audience. In 1920, the Marconi Company broadcast the first British radio programme and, suddenly, everyone wanted a wireless in their home. Before the invention of television, radio was the main form of home entertainment and also kept people up-to-date with world news.

## IN THE MODERN WORLD

Today, all these methods of communication have moved forward in ways which their inventors could never have imagined. Radio is used as a method of communication for shipping, aircraft, the armed forces and emergency services such as the police. Radio now spans distances undreamt of by Marconi.

and people have telephones in their cars and mobile phones that can be charged up so that they work without wires. A telephone which shows a picture of the caller and recipient on a small screen is now becoming available.

The most exciting development of all came when people began to link computers together using telephone lines, to create the internet. This began with experiments in the USA in the late 1960s, when a small number of machines were linked up. Now the internet links

Communications satellites have made it possible to link up distant corners of the world and even to communicate with craft in space.

Today, most people have a telephone in their home, but at the beginning of the century, the newly invented telephone was a luxury few people could afford. The telephone can link people on opposite sides of the world in seconds,

millions of computers all over the world, allowing users to share information and communicate with each other by email. The net makes electronic commerce possible, enables you to play games online and is endlessly useful for research. In addition, sound files, pictures and movies can be sent via the net. The world of communications has been transformed.

# RECORDING SOUND

*From the first crackling records
to today's superb quality compact discs,
sound recording has brought
pleasure to millions.*

The nineteenth century was a time of great change, and inventors came up with a whole range of new ideas. One of these was the concept of storing sounds on a solid material so that they could be played over and over again. The first machine for recording and reproducing sounds was invented in 1877, by an American, Thomas Alva Edison (1847–1931), one of the greatest inventors of the nineteenth century.

In 1876, Edison set up his own research laboratory at Menlo Park near New York. The following year, he invented the phonograph for recording and playing back sound. He got the idea from the telephone which had recently been invented. He knew that the mouthpiece and earpiece of the telephone contained discs which vibrated in response to the human voice. Edison saw that he could connect a needle to a mouthpiece with a vibrating disc. If he spoke into the mouthpiece, the disc would vibrate and

△ *The tiny personal stereo, so often used today, produces a far better sound than the enormous gramophones of the early twentieth century.*

the needle would cut a groove into a solid material in the pattern of the sound vibrations. A second needle fitted to the vibrating disc in the earpiece of the instrument would then convert the sounds and play them back. In July 1877, Edison tried out his idea. He constructed a recording machine and shouted the word 'hello' into it. The sound that came back to him was an indistinct, but definite, 'hello'.

## A MECHANICAL EAR

Edison now set about making a more permanent recording machine which he called a 'phonograph'. A needle was attached to a thin skin, or membrane. This membrane was stretched across the narrow end of a horn, rather like the eardrum at the end of the ear canal. The horn collected up the sounds and channelled them to the membrane, in the same way that the ear flap collects sounds and channels them to the eardrum.

When Edison spoke into the horn, the membrane vibrated with the sound of his voice. With each vibration, the needle cut tiny marks into a sheet of tin foil wrapped around a revolving cylinder. As the cylinder turned, the needle made a pattern of marks in a continuous spiral. It cut into the foil at different depths for different sound vibrations. This is called 'hill-and-dale' recording because the groove is like a series of hills and valleys.

To play the recording back, the needle moved

◁ *Thomas Alva Edison*

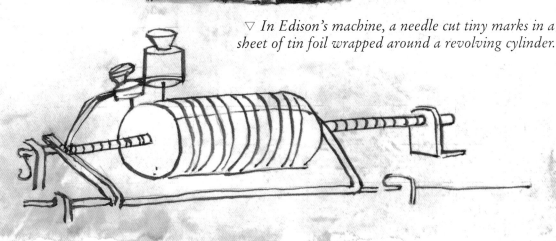

▽ *In Edison's machine, a needle cut tiny marks in a sheet of tin foil wrapped around a revolving cylinder.*

along the spiral groove. The indentations in the foil made the needle and membrane vibrate in different ways, and the sound recording was heard through the horn. Edison's first recording was the nursery rhyme 'Mary had a little lamb'.

Edison's invention brought him world-wide fame, but his phonograph was very basic. The sound quality was not good and the cylinders did not last long. However, Edison was more interested in thinking up new ideas than in perfecting his inventions and it was left to others to improve on the phonograph. In 1886,

a machine called a 'graphophone' was invented. It was similar to the phonograph but used a wax cylinder instead of tin foil, and a cutter shaped like a chisel instead of a needle. This gave better sound quality than Edison's machine.

## THE FIRST DISCS

In 1887, Emile Berliner (1851–1929), a German living in America, came up with a long-lasting idea: the record. Berliner's record was a flat disc made of zinc covered with a layer of wax. A cutter made a spiral groove in the wax,

▽ On the phonograph, the person spoke into the horn to make a recording. The horn also amplified the sounds when they were played back. This worked reasonably well for recording a single person talking or singing but it was not so good for recording several people such as a group of musicians.

but instead of up-and-down indentations like hills and valleys, it cut a wavy groove which ran from side-to-side along the surface. This method, known as 'lateral' recording, reproduced sounds more accurately than the hill-and-dale method. When the groove had been cut into the wax, acid was used to etch it into the metal disc. This created a permanent master copy from which other copies could be made. Flat discs could be pressed so that both sides of the record were stamped at once which made them far easier to copy than cylinders.

*Emile Berliner invented the disc-shaped record.*

The records had to be copied on to a soft material which set hard. Early records were made from shellac, a natural plastic made from the secretions of the lac insect which is found on some trees in India and Thailand. Later, shellac was replaced by vinyl plastic.

Having found a way to make records, Berliner went on to design a machine for playing them; the 'gramophone'. The early gramophone had a large horn for making the record sound louder. The machine had to be wound up with a handle to make the turntable revolve.

## LOUDER AND CLEARER

The sound on a gramophone with a horn was crackly and not very realistic. The next big improvement was to introduce a microphone and loudspeaker into the gramophone. There are various different types of microphone, but they are all used to change sound into a varying electric current.

One of the earliest microphones was invented in 1878 for use in the telephone. This is known as the 'carbon' microphone.

Vibrating discs in the telephone form the lids of two small containers filled with grains of carbon. When someone talks into it, each disc, or 'diaphragm', vibrates as the carbon moves in the container.

The speed of the vibrations depends on the pitch of the person's voice, that is, how high or low it is. The amount of vibration depends on the volume of the voice. When the diaphragm moves inwards, the grains of carbon are packed tightly together. This allows more electricity to flow through the carbon. When the diaphragm moves outwards, the grains are packed more loosely and less electricity flows through. So a varying sequence of electrical signals is passed down the wire.

## THE MOVING COIL

The microphone used for recording is the 'moving-coil' microphone. A thin disc of metal vibrates when sounds hit it. Attached to the metal is a coil of wire which also moves. A magnet produces an electric current in the wire. The strength of the current varies depending on the pitch and volume of the sounds.

A machine with a microphone also needs a loudspeaker to play back the sounds. A loudspeaker has a motor which usually consists of a coil of wire moving near a magnet. The electric current from the microphone is fed into the motor, and the signals cause a diaphragm to vibrate. The vibrations make the air around them vibrate too, and this reaches our ears as

△ *Tiny variations in the groove of a record cause the stylus to vibrate in different ways. The vibrations of the stylus are then amplified to produce a copy of the original sound.*

the recorded sounds. The signals from a microphone are very weak and have to be strengthened by an amplifier before they are passed to the loudspeaker.

Early microphone and loudspeaker systems were not nearly as sophisticated as those we have now, but even the earliest versions greatly improved the quality of sound recordings.

## TAPE RECORDERS

The earliest type of magnetic tape recording was patented in 1898 – it stored electrical signals on magnetized steel wire. However, the idea did not catch on because there was so much electrical interference that it was hard to make out

what the sounds were meant to be. A better type of tape was introduced in the United States in 1927. This was a strip of paper covered in a liquid containing very tiny iron filings. When the liquid dried, the iron filings remained on the surface. As the tape moved past the 'record head' during recording, electric currents magnetized the iron dust. The strength of the current varied depending on the sounds being picked up and so created a magnetized pattern on the tape.

When the tape was played back, another magnet called the 'playback head' converted this pattern into the recorded sounds. This system was developed in Britain, the United States and Germany during the 1930s. By 1936, it was efficient enough to use for the first tape recording of a concert orchestra in Berlin.

Early tape recorders were large machines known as 'reel-to-reel' tapes. Each tape was wound on to a single large spool. To use the tape, the loose end had to be threaded past the magnetic heads and wound on to a second 'take-up' spool. Reel-to-reel tape recordings are still used for some things, such as professional sound recordings, but a more modern idea for home use is the cassette tape recorder, which was first introduced in 1961. The tape is mounted on two small spools inside a plastic case, the cassette. The whole cassette is pushed into the machine to record or play the tape.

## HI-FI SOUND

Today, people can listen to the music of a complete orchestra with the sound of each instrument faithfully reproduced. The accuracy of a recording is known as the 'fidelity'. Equipment which produces high quality and accurate sound reproduction is known as high-fidelity or 'hi-fi' equipment.

Most music is now produced using 'stereophonic' or 'stereo' sound. Several microphones are used to record the music. Each microphone is fitted to a separate amplifier on a control desk and picks up a different aspect of the music. The recorded music is played back through two or more speakers.

Stereo gives the effect that the music is spread out in front of you. 'Surround sound', played back through five or six speakers, goes a step further to create the kind of effect you hear in the cinema.

▽ *A vast range of equipment for recording and playing back sound is available today.*

## DIGITAL RECORDING

The latest method of reproducing music is digital recording, which was introduced in the 1980s. Sound is stored as a digital code which is translated into a sound by a computerized player. The compact disc, or CD, is the best known form of digital sound recording. It is a thin plastic disc covered with a shiny protective coating. The surface of the disc is covered with an arrangement of very tiny pits in a special code. When the disc is played in a CD player, a laser beam reads the code and changes it into electrical signals which are then played as sounds. Compact discs produce the finest-quality sound available at the moment. There is no crackling and manufacturers claim that they do not wear out, however much you play them.

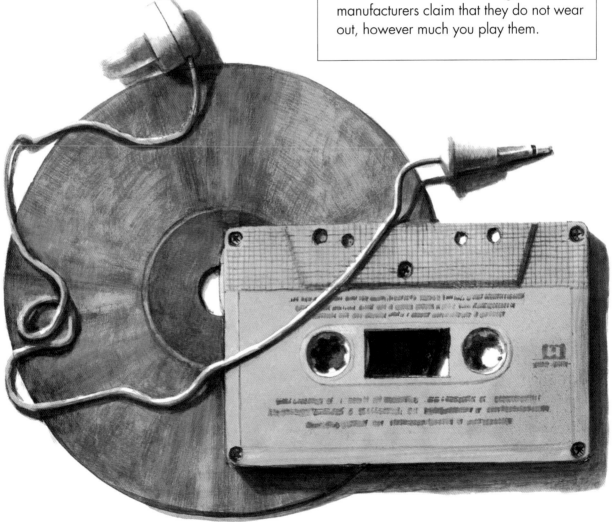

# MOVING IMAGES

*We think of moving pictures as a very modern invention, but the first steps towards today's films, television and videos were taken over 150 years ago.*

hen you go to see a film or watch television, you are witnessing the inventions of many different people. We take these ideas for granted today, but, in the nineteenth and early twentieth century, the concept of moving pictures was very new and exciting. The idea of moving pictures actually came before photography had been invented.

△ *Early cameras were bulky to carry about and difficult to set up.*

One of film's ancestors was the magic lantern, invented in 1654. This was a way of using light to show still pictures. In 1829, a French scientist, Joseph Antoine Ferdinand Plateau (1801–83), worked out the theory which forms the basis of moving images. His intention was to prove that the eye can be tricked into seeing something that is not accurate.

An action such as running is broken down into a sequence of step-by-step pictures. The pictures are then played back at the same speed as the original movement. Because the human eye retains each image for about one-thirtieth of a second, the pictures all merge in the viewer's mind and create the illusion of movement. In 1832, Plateau made a device called a 'phenakistiscope' to demonstrate his theory. A revolving cardboard disc contained the sequence of pictures showing each tiny stage of a movement. Each of the pictures was revealed to the viewer in turn, giving the impression that the image was moving.

## CAPTURING AN IMAGE

These early moving pictures were hand-drawn images. But the development of photography was to have a huge impact on the idea of moving pictures. To make

### THE CAMERA OBSCURA

The principle on which photography is based had been known since ancient times. A beam of light coming into a darkened room through a small hole in one wall will project a reversed, upside-down image of the scene outside on the opposite wall. Archimedes (c. 287–212 BC), the Greek mathematician and inventor, knew of this principle, known as the 'camera obscura', Greek for 'dark room'. The Arab scholar al-Haytham (965–1038) used it to watch eclipses of the Sun, and Leonardo da Vinci (1452–1519) described the principle in great detail. The camera obscura was first used to project temporary, hand-drawn images in the late sixteenth century.

a photograph, a projected image had to be captured on a substance which could retain it permanently. People had known how to project images for centuries, so they only needed to discover how to fix the image. Scientists knew that silver nitrate turned black when it was exposed to the light, so at the beginning of the nineteenth century, several people experimented with using silver salts to fix images on paper. In 1802, the first images were produced on paper coated in silver nitrate, but the pictures quickly faded.

A Frenchman, Joseph Niepce (1765–1833), was the first person to capture a permanent image. He began to experiment in 1816 and, after many attempts, he managed to make a picture on a sheet of paper coated with silver chloride at the back of a camera obscura. However, the image was a negative with all the tones reversed. He did not succeed in making a print from his negative, but instead concentrated on finding a way of making a positive image straightaway. In 1826, he finally managed to produce a picture on a metal plate.

The following year, Niepce met another Frenchman, Louis-Jacques-Mandé Daguerre (1787–1851), and the two began to work together. In 1835, Daguerre perfected a process of producing an image on a metal plate. The quality of his 'daguerreotypes' was exceptional, and they became very fashionable during the 1840s and 1850s.

## A PERMANENT PRINT

It was William Henry Fox Talbot (1800–77) who made the most significant step towards modern photography.

Fox Talbot wrestled for six years with the problem of converting a negative to a permanent print on paper. In 1839, he at last managed to obtain a positive print on paper.

As techniques improved, photography became more popular. In 1871, a young American amateur photographer, George Eastman (1854–1932), invented a machine for efficient developing of photographic plates and founded the Eastman Dry Plate Company, which later became the world famous Kodak. In 1888, Eastman revolutionized photography with the Kodak box camera, which was light and simple to use. For the first time, anyone could take photographs without setting up complicated equipment.

*Eadweard Muybridge*

used his invention to photograph the flight of seagulls on the seashore in Naples, where the locals commented on the crazy man who aimed a gun at birds without ever shooting any!

Now the possibilities began to interest the great American inventor, Thomas Edison. He began discussions with Muybridge about combining his phonograph with the 'Zoopraxiscope', a machine which Muybridge had designed for projecting his photographic sequences.

In 1888, Edison's team at Menlo Park came up with their own device for viewing films, which they called the

## THE PICTURES MOVE

Meanwhile, other people had seen how photography could play a part in producing moving images. A step-by-step sequence of photographs could show movements far more accurately than drawings.

The main pioneer of action photography was Eadweard Muybridge (1830–1904). Muybridge took endless pictures of moving animals and people, and proved, with one of his step-by-step series, that a galloping horse lifts all four legs off the ground at the same time, a fact that no-one had realized before.

Another photographer working on movement shots was a Frenchman, Etienne Jules Marey (1830–1904). In 1882, he invented a photographic rifle that allowed him to take a series of photographs very rapidly. Marey

'Kinetoscope'. They used a camera like Marey's to make the films, but they introduced an important improvement which is still used to this day. Marey had found it difficult to move the film smoothly through the camera. Edison's team used film with holes along the edges. As the film wound on, the holes engaged with a sprocket in the camera and the playback machine.

The kinetoscope was a wooden box containing a battery-powered motor, a lamp, a magnifying lens, and an eyepiece. Only one person could watch the film at a time, peering through the eyepiece as the film flickered past the lamp.

The quality of these early films was very poor. To improve it, Edison opened the first movie studio, an open-topped shed on wheels. It had large windows and could be moved around to follow the sun, so that the scenes being played inside were always well-lit.

People were intrigued by moving pictures and, in the 1890s, they became a popular attraction. Peepshow parlours began to appear, where people could peer into kinetoscopes and marvel at the moving images.

## DRAWING THE CROWDS

The interest in films inspired other people to improve on Edison's equipment. An obvious development was to find a way of showing a film on a big screen so that a crowd of people could watch it at the same time. Edison started to work on some ideas, but soon lost interest. It was left to two French brothers, Louis (1864–1948) and Auguste (1862–1954) Lumière, to develop the ancestor of the movie projector.

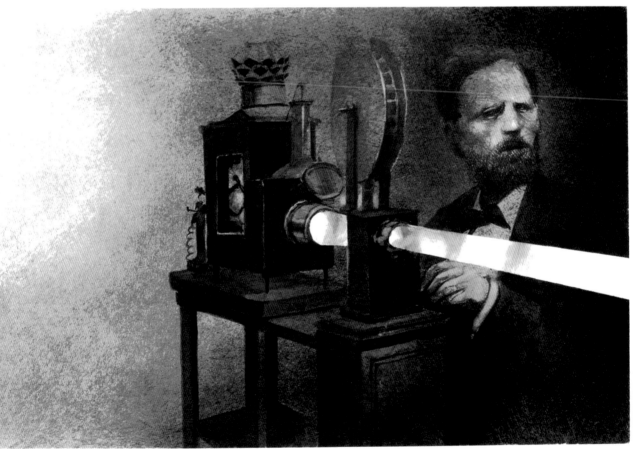

△ *Edison's kinetoscope and the Lumières' equipment.*

The Lumière brothers ran a factory producing photographic equipment in Lyons, France. They began to take an interest in motion pictures, and in 1894, they set to work to improve on Edison's kinetoscope. On 13 February 1895, they

◁ *Walt Disney using a Pathé camera.*

## STEP-BY-STEP TO MOVING PICTURES

**1826** Niepce produces the first photograph on a metal plate.

**1829** Plateau puts forward his 'persistence of vision' theory.

**1839** Fox Talbot discovers the negative/positive process and prints a photograph on paper.

**1878** Muybridge produces a sequence of photographs showing that a horse lifts all of its feet when it gallops.

**1882** Marey invents a photographic rifle for action shots.

**1884** Nipkow invents the scanning disc.

**1888** Edison's team patents the Kinetoscope.

**1895** The Lumière brothers give the first public cinema show in Paris.

**1897** Pathé invents a separate camera and projector.

**1923** Zworykin demonstrates the conversion of an image into electrical signals.

**1926** Baird gives the first public demonstration of television.

**1929** The BBC begins to broadcast television programmes in Britain.

**1937** Baird's system is dropped by the BBC in favour of Marconi-EMI's electronic equipment.

patented their invention, which they called the 'cinematograph'. For the rest of that year, they gave private film shows to arouse interest in their work. On 28 December 1895, they gave their first film show to a paying audience, in a makeshift cinema in the basement of a Paris cafe.

These early films were not very exciting. The Lumières' first film showed workers leaving their factory in Lyons, and another showed a baby eating breakfast. On the other hand, some of their films were more exciting. One film showed a train coming into a station and was shot at such an angle that the audience were terrified that the train was actually going to hit them.

But the main thing was that the pictures moved. The novelty was so great that audiences flocked to see anything.

By 1897, the Lumières had made 358 short films. By 1901, there were 1,299.

Other people soon followed the Lumière brothers and began to make film equipment. A Frenchman, Charles Pathé (1867–1957), invented a separate camera and projector in 1897, and then set up a company to make films. The film craze spread from France to America, where a huge film industry quickly began to grow. Many people contributed to the growth of this industry, including the famous Walt Disney (1901–66) who is perhaps best known for cartoons, such as Mickey Mouse, first designed in 1928.

## THE INVENTION OF TELEVISION

The discovery that sounds could travel by radio waves set several scientists thinking. If sounds could be transmitted in this way, what about pictures?

The main problem was how to convert a picture into a continuous sequence of information, a process called scanning. When you look at a picture on a television screen, you are seeing millions of tiny dots of light. These dots are arranged in lines, like the lines in a book. On a modern television, the picture has 625 lines. The more lines the picture has, the more detailed and precise it can be, because the image is broken up into very tiny parts.

Before a television programme can be transmitted, these spots of light have to be converted into electrical signals which can be sent out on electromagnetic radio waves. This conversion is made in the television camera. The television set is a receiver. The aerial picks up the signals. The cathode ray tube in the television converts the signals into pictures, and the speaker produces the sounds.

Some of the first pioneers of television looked at electronic methods. In 1923, a

△ *The famous comic actor Charlie Chaplin (1889–1977) made his first film in 1913 and was an immediate success with his character, the tramp in baggy trousers and bowler hat. Chaplin became one of the great stars of the early silent films.*

Russian-born American, Vladimir Zworykin (1889–1982) developed a procedure for converting an image into electrical signals.

## SCANNING THE IMAGE

Meanwhile, another pioneer was developing television in quite a different way. John Logie Baird (1888–1946) was a Scottish engineer-turned-inventor. He had been struggling with unsuccessful inventions for nine years when, one day in 1923, he came up with an idea for a mechanical scanning system. It was based on an 1884 invention by a German student, Paul Nipkow (1860–1940). Nipkow had had the idea of cutting up images into lines. He produced an 'electric telescope' which consisted of a disc pierced with a spiral of holes. When the disc spun in front of an object, it divided the object into a series of lines.

△ *John Logie Baird*

▷ *Baird's clumsy contraption used a spinning disc with holes round the edge to break an image up into lines.*

## A FLICKERING IMAGE

Baird applied for a patent to use Nipkow's disc to make a television with a mechanical system of scanning. He used old radio parts and other bits and pieces to make a clumsy transmitter, and, in 1925, he managed to produce a flickering, shadowy picture.

Greatly excited by his success, Baird borrowed money to improve his equipment and rented an attic workshop in London. In 1926, he televised a ventriloquist's dummy at a public demonstration in his workshop. The image was made up of only eight lines so it was very dim and blurred. But, despite the poor quality of the picture, the demonstration was a great success. Like the first films, the idea of a television was so new that any success seemed like a miracle. People became very excited by the possibilities of this new communication system.

Baird set up his own company to work on improving the quality of his pictures. The BBC had been founded in 1922 to broadcast radio programmes, and in 1929 Baird persuaded them to transmit a television service.

Meanwhile, other companies were working on the electronic methods begun by Zworykin and others. In 1933,

Zworykin patented the 'iconoscope', a camera tube that converted an image into electrical pulses. It was used by the RCA (Radio Corporation of America) for experimental broadcasts in 1936. In Britain, the Marconi Company and EMI (Electrical Musical Instruments) were working on improved television systems.

## BETTER QUALITY PICTURES

The equipment they came up with was more sophisticated than Baird's mechanical device, which had several drawbacks. The camera was fixed in position so anyone being televised had to stay in one position. The quality of the picture was so bad that people being televised had to wear clown-like make-up so that their features showed up, and the flickering light from the machine almost blinded them. The last straw was that Baird's system kept on breaking down.

*△ Despite the very poor quality of the picture he produced, Baird's invention caused great excitement when he demonstrated it at his workshop in Soho, London, in 1926.*

The BBC now had enough choice to set higher standards for their programmes. Baird invented a 240-line mechanically scanned system which was an improvement, but Marconi-EMI introduced a 405-line system with electronic scanning. For a while, the BBC used both systems for their programmes, but in 1937, they finally dropped Baird's system in favour of the electronic method.

Baird was bitterly disappointed by this rejection. However, even though other pioneers were working on ideas and introducing more sophisticated equipment than Baird's, those first flickering pictures he produced in 1925 earned him credit as the inventor of television.

# FIND OUT SOME MORE

After you have read about the ideas and inventions in this book, you may want to find out some more information about them. There are lots of books devoted to specific topics, such as printing or photography, so that you can discover more facts. All over Britain and Ireland, you can see historical sites and visit museums that contain historical artefacts that will tell you more about the subjects that interest you. The books, sites and museums listed below cover some of the most important topics in this book. They are just a start!

## GENERAL INFORMATION

BOOKS

These books all present a large number of inventions of all different kinds:

*Oxford Illustrated Encyclopedia of Invention and Technology* edited by Sir Monty Finniston (Oxford University Press, 1992)

*Usborne Illustrated Handbook of Invention and Discovery* by Struan Reid (Usborne, 1986)

*Invention* by Lionel Bender (Dorling Kindersley, 1986)

*The Way Things Work* by David Macaulay (Dorling Kindersley, 1988)

*Key Moments in Science and Technology* by Keith Wicks (Hamlyn, 1999)

*A History of Invention* by Trevor I. Williams (Little Brown, 1999)

WEBSITE

For information on many different inventions, visit: http://inventors.about.com

MUSEUMS

Many large museums contain interesting artefacts related to people of the past, and some have collections that may be more specifically about some of the themes covered in this book.

To find out more about the museums in your area, ask in your local library or tourist information office, or look in the telephone directory.

A useful guide is *Museums & Galleries in Great Britain & Ireland* (British Leisure Publications, East Grinstead) which tells you about over 1,300 places to visit. For a good introduction to the subjects covered in this book, visit:

**Science Museum**, Exhibition Road, London SW7
www.sciencemuseum.org.uk

For displays and information about many of the earliest ideas and inventions, go to:

**British Museum**, Great Russell Street, London WC1
www.britishmuseum.co.uk

## WRITING & BOOKS

BOOKS

*Writing* by Karen Brookfield (Dorling Kindersley, 1993)

MUSEUMS

Many museums and libraries contain interesting examples of different scripts and writing materials used in the past.

In the **British Museum**, London (address above) you can see the Rosetta Stone as well as scripts, old illuminated manuscripts and examples of papyri. There are also fascinating displays of all sorts of writing at:

**The British Library**, 96 Euston Road, London NW1
www.bl.uk

WEBSITES

These two websites cover the history of writing and scripts:
www.historian.net/hxwrite.htm
www.quillandmouse.com/qm0798.htm

## PHOTOGRAPHY, FILM AND TV

BOOKS

*Cinema* by Richard Platt (Dorling Kindersley, 1992)

MUSEUMS

**National Museum of Photography, Film and Television**, Prince's View, Bradford, West Yorkshire
www.nmpft.org.uk

**Royal Photographic Society**, Milsom Street, Bath, Avon. Presents the history of photography from Niepce to the present.
www.rps.org

WEBSITE

For more about the history of TV, visit:
www.tvhistory.tv

## RADIO

WEBSITE

There is lots of information about the story of radio at:
www.history.acusd.edu/gen/recording/radio.html

## INTERNET

WEBSITE

There is a short history of the internet at:
www.isoc.org/internet/history/brief.shtml

# INDEX